MADELYN MAKES POTTERY

BY JOHN BRUCE

Bianca Bruce

Zebulon Pottery

To my daughter, Madelyn.
Be brave enough to walk your own path, find creative solutions, and have fun doing it.

MADELYN makes POTTERY

By John Bruce

Madelyn wants some juice, but cannot find a mug her size.

Creative
Juice

She has a bright idea to make her own.

EENY . . . . MEENIE . . .

She gets the perfect amount of clay
for her project.

ONE, TWO...
PICK A FEW

She collects the right tools to help shape the clay.

Madelyn shapes and pulls the clay making sure to get everything just right for her!

She pulls and bends the handle,

and makes sure it's a perfect fit.

GLAZE

She paints glaze on her mug so it will be shiny and beautiful.

She washes her hands so she doesn't make a mess.

Madelyn helps her dad unload the kiln.

Juice

She pours
juice into her perfectly sized mug.

She loves drinking out of her new mug,
and enjoys all of her hard work.

She doesn't know what she'll do tomorrow, but Madelyn knows she will always find a way to be creative.

POTTERY STUDIO

SLIP

Did you find all of the kiln gremlins?

Kiln gremlins are creatures who cause a little bit of mischief in the pottery studio. They live in the kiln, and sneak out to play tricks on potters.

A Human Tradition

Making pottery is one of the oldest and enduring crafts that people do. It has been around for thousands of years, and some of the oldest pottery found dates back over 10,000 years.
Making pottery that you eat or drink out of is one of the oldest human traditions from all over the world.
If you ever get to make your own pottery, you will
join the amazing legacy of potters before you and help keep the tradition alive!

Modern Pottery Process

1. A potter gathers clay, and makes a piece of unique pottery. Hand building, throwing on the wheel, and slip casting are the main ways to make pottery.

2. The pottery dries out for a few days, and then goes into the kiln to be fired. The first firing is called a bisque firing. This is where the clay becomes ceramic.

3. The potter paints or dips the pottery in glaze.

4. The pottery goes into the kiln one more time. This is called the glaze firing.

5. The pottery is now ready to use!

Madelyn Makes Pottery

First Printing, 2023

Contact the author at
Zebulonpottery.com

www.ingramcontent.com/pod-product-compliance
Ingram Content Group UK Ltd.
Pitfield, Milton Keynes, MK11 3LW, UK
UKHW061031310726
14089UKWH00009B/186
9798218284008